MARY FORD'S
CHOCOLATE COOKBOOK

WITH STEP-BY-STEP INSTRUCTIONS

ACKNOWLEDGEMENT

Mary Ford acknowledges with grateful thanks the assistance of Jean Baker in compiling this book.

MARY FORD TUBE NUMBERS SHOWING THEIR SHAPES

1   •   2   ●   7   ✸   42   ●   43   ✸   44   ✸

The above are all the icing tubes used in this book. Please note that these are Mary Ford Tube Numbers, but comparable tubes may be used. Most of the equipment, including moulds, required to complete the confections in this book can be obtained from the Mary Ford Cake Artistry Centre, 28-30 Southbourne Grove, Bournemouth, Dorset, BH6 3RA, England, or local stockists.

OTHER MARY FORD TITLES

101 CAKE DESIGNS
ANOTHER 101 CAKE DESIGNS
THE CONCISE BOOK OF CAKE MAKING AND DECORATING
SUGARPASTE CAKE DECORATING
WRITING IN ICING
PARTY CAKES
MAKING CAKES FOR MONEY
MAKING SOFT TOYS
MAKING GLOVE PUPPETS
SUGAR FLOWERS CAKE DECORATING
A CAKE FOR ALL SEASONS

ISBN 0 946429 18 9

Published by Mary Ford Publications Limited, 294b Lymington Road, Highcliffe on Sea, Christchurch, Dorset BH23 5ET.

Printed and bound in Hong Kong.

Contents

Author

Mary Ford is renowned for her cake decoration and creative skills. She has spent a lifetime working in the confectionery trade and has extensive experience in chocolate craft. Her pictorial cake artistry books have won world wide acclaim bringing her unique step-by-step teaching method to a wide audience. Mary's personal warmth and charm have endeared her to a generation of students and cakemakers alike.

Mary's husband, Michael, works closely with Mary in planning and producing all her books. All the photographs are taken by him in their studio in England. He is also responsible for editing the books.

Introduction

Chocolate is one of the most luxurious tastes known to man and in this delicious new book Mary Ford shares her expertise in this versatile medium and introduces an exciting range of luscious cakes and gateaux, rich biscuits, indulgent sweets and attractive Easter eggs. The pictorial format includes detailed, step-by-step instructions for creating sumptuous confections to a very high standard with a minimum of difficulty.

An introductory section clearly shows all the preparatory steps necessary and includes Mary Ford's own Hints and Tips for professional results. Beginners will find that, by familiarising themselves with the information contained in this section, mistakes will be avoided and the work will proceed smoothly to a perfect finish.

This exciting and versatile cookbook for the chocolate enthusiast is divided into sections and forms a structured course in chocolate confections. Following the introductory section, the art of sweet-making is explained in easy-to-follow step-by-step photographs. The next pictorial section then covers the making and decorating of moulded forms to produce delightful, handmade Easter Eggs. The second part of the book contains a delicious range of cakes, gateaux and luxury desserts.

The wickedly seductive taste of rich, smooth chocolate is irresistible and this book offers you the opportunity to indulge yourself to the full whilst learning the practical skills of chocolate cookery. It is a book to conjure up luscious fantasies, offering sensuous gastronomic experiences for the whole family, or wonderful presents for favoured friends.

All About Chocolate

Compound chocolate (otherwise known as chocolate flavoured covering, baker's chocolate or trade names such as Scotbloc) or couverture chocolate can be used for all the products in this book. It is important to temper couverture before using for moulds, sweets or dipping as specified in the recipes.

NOTE: WHEN MAKING ANY OF THE RECIPES IN THIS BOOK, FOLLOW ONE SET OF MEASUREMENTS ONLY AS THEY ARE NOT INTERCHANGEABLE.

The History of Chocolate

THE Aztecs called chocolate 'The Food of the Gods' and for them drinking ceremonial chocolate was a sacred experience. At the court of Emperor Montezuma a frothy chocolate concoction was drunk out of ornate golden goblets and the highly prized cocoa beans were used as currency. On one of Christopher Columbus's journeys to the New World he saw the natives drinking chocolate and brought back some cocoa beans but it was left to Hernando Cortez, during his conquest of Mexico, to realise the true value. He set up a cocoa plantation and exported the beans to his native Spain where it was drunk as a bitter brew to which spices were added to improve the flavour.

Eventually, however, sugar was added to make the drink more palatable and it became a favourite beverage. It was a highly exclusive drink at that time, restricted to the Spanish grandees, and it was not until almost a century later that a Spanish princess took the treasured drink with her to France where it became a favourite at the Court. By the eighteenth century it had become so popular that the fashionable Coffee Houses began to serve it to their customers.

At the end of the eighteenth century Dr Joseph Fry began to manufacture chocolate on a large scale using a steam engine to grind the beans. It was, however, still used mostly as a beverage and it was not until the end of the nineteenth century that a Swiss manufacturer, Daniel Peter, finally succeeded in adding condensed milk to make a solid milk chocolate. A little while later Rodolphe Lindt perfected a method of preparation which brought chocolate to the smooth confection with which we are familiar today.

THE WORLD'S FAVOURITE FLAVOUR

FOR versatility and appeal, nothing beats the flavour of chocolate for cooking, and it is a universal favourite. Chocolate is manufactured from the product of pressed, roasted cocoa beans. A liquid paste, called 'chocolate liquor', is the main ingredient of the different types of 'chocolate' available. When combined with cocoa butter as the fat content, this can be legally described as 'chocolate' and is known as couverture. Vegetable fat can also be incorporated to form a compound chocolate often known as chocolate flavoured covering, baker's chocolate, or other chocolate products sold under trade names.

Couverture Chocolate

COUVERTURE is the purest form of chocolate and it is recommended for all the products in this book. It is well worth the extra effort and time involved in 'tempering' (see page 8) as it has a superior flavour to compound chocolate. Couverture is less sweet and the high fat content (minimum 30%) gives it a smooth, attractive, and glossy appearance, making it ideal for mould work as well as for coating sweets and chocolates.

Couverture chocolate can be purchased from most confectioners or specialist shops in the form of a high quality 'block of chocolate' in milk, plain or white varieties. Plain couverture has a strong, bitter flavour and is available in sweetened or unsweetened form. Milk couverture has a lighter, sweeter flavour because, as its name suggests, milk is incorporated into the manufacturing process. White chocolate is produced from a combination of cocoa butter, sugar and milk.

Couverture must first be 'tempered' (see page 8) when used for moulds and sweet-dipping in order to bring the chocolate to a crystalline state, ensuring a hard, brittle surface and a good shelf life. However it is not always necessary to temper couverture before use and the recipes in this book all clearly state whether or not tempering is required. Tempering will also reduce the risk of 'bloom', a greyish-white film resulting from crystals rising to the surface after exposure to varying temperatures or excessive moisture. It is for this reason that couverture should never be kept in a refrigerator.

Because milk and white couverture soften more readily than plain, it is important to keep the temperatures 1°C (2°F) lower at all stages during the tempering of milk based couverture.

Compound Chocolate

COMPOUND chocolate, otherwise known as chocolate flavoured covering, baker's chocolate, or other chocolate products sold under trade names such as Scotbloc, is available in most supermarkets in the form of slabs or buttons. It has as its main ingredient a good quality vegetable fat and includes sugar, milk powder, cocoa solids in the form of cocoa powder, and emulsifiers such as lecithin (found in soya beans).

Compound chocolate is extremely easy to use as, unlike couverture, it does not require tempering and can be melted easily over a pan of hot water (see page 9).

Special diet or diabetic chocolate, which does not contain sugar, is also readily available, but this is only recommended in cases of special need. It should be melted carefully over warm water and does not require tempering.

CAROB
Carob is a caffeine-free alternative to chocolate which is widely available in health food stores. Made from the pods of the carob tree, carob is available as a powder or as plain or flavoured bars. Some carob products are entirely milk free making them suitable for use by vegans or those on a lactose-free diet.

Carob bars should be melted over hot water and do not need tempering. The appearance of carob confections is not as attractive as that of chocolate as it has a dull finish. However, this can be improved by the addition of 15ml (1tbsp) of skimmed milk powder diluted in hot water to the carob, which produces a more glossy appearance.

COCOA POWDER
Cocoa powder is made from dried cocoa butter and it has a bitter taste. It is the most economical chocolate flavouring for cakes and icing. Drinking chocolate is cocoa to which sugar has been added to give a milder, sweeter flavour.

Tempering Couverture Chocolate

NOTE: *Do not use this method for compound chocolate.*

TEMPERING couverture is essential in order to bring it to a crystalline state which will produce a high gloss finish, a hard surface and a good 'snap' when broken. Inadequate tempering results in a blotchy, streaky and generally poor finish which does not set well. It may also produce an unattractive bloom on the surface of the couverture.

Tempering, which involves raising, lowering, and then raising the temperature of the couverture again, to very precise degrees, takes about thirty to forty minutes for 455g (16oz) of couverture. The exact length of time will depend on the warmth of the room where the tempering is done, which ideally should be around 18-19°C (65-67°F). The reason for tempering couverture is to make sure that the cocoa-butter is distributed evenly. If the couverture becomes too hot, the cocoa-butter floats to the top and sets, producing a streaky surface. If the temperature is too low, the chocolate sets to a greyish-white colour.

When tempering milk couverture, the temperatures should be 1°C (2°F) lower at all stages than for plain couverture. Tempered plain couverture should be kept at a temperature of 31°C (88°F) and milk couverture at a temperature of 30°C (86°F).

HOW TO TEMPER COUVERTURE:
1 *Break plain couverture chocolate into small pieces and place in heat-proof bowl.*

2 *Stand the bowl over a pan of simmering, not boiling, water and stir until the chocolate is melted.*

3 *Heat and stir the chocolate slowly until a temperature of 46°C (115°F) is reached.* **Reduce all temperatures by 1°C (2°F) for milk couverture chocolate.**

4 *Remove the bowl from the heat and stand it in cold water. Stir the chocolate until it cools to 27-28°C (80-82°F).*

5 *Return the bowl to the saucepan until the temperature of the chocolate reaches 31°C (88°F). Remove from the heat.*

6 *Test a small amount of chocolate on greaseproof paper. If it does not set within 5 minutes, repeat steps 3-5. Keep the chocolate at 31°C (88°F) whilst in use.*

How to melt Compound Chocolate

HOW TO MELT COMPOUND CHOCOLATE

THE method shown below is a quick and easy way to melt chocolate flavoured covering, baker's chocolate or chocolate substitutes such as carob.

NOTE: *This method can also be followed to melt couverture used in recipes which specify that it does not require tempering.*

A double-boiler saucepan should preferably be used as this prevents scorching, but alternatively a heat-proof bowl can be used over an ordinary saucepan which is small enough to support the bowl without it touching the base. The water level should not be allowed to touch the bowl.

MELTING COMPOUND CHOCOLATE IN A MICROWAVE

To melt 225g (8oz) of plain chocolate in a microwave, place broken pieces, or buttons, in a non-metallic bowl and microwave for 4-5 minutes on a medium setting, stirring once. Times are based on a 650W microwave oven. Individual ovens will vary, so check during heating. Milk chocolate will need slightly less time.

When just softened, remove from the microwave and stir well until the chocolate has completely melted. It is important not to overheat beyond the point where the chocolate is just soft, as this makes it grainy and unmanageable.

HOW TO MELT COMPOUND CHOCOLATE OR COUVERTURE (see note above)

1 Working in a cool room temperature, place broken pieces, or buttons, into a heat-proof bowl.

2 Stand the bowl over a pan of simmering, not boiling, water and stir until the chocolate is almost melted.

3 Remove from heat and continue stirring until chocolate is smooth and completely melted. Keep it warm, stirring occasionally, to prevent it from setting while in use.

Moulding Chocolate

Moulds are available in many different shapes and sizes, and are made in a variety of materials. Plastic moulds are ideal as they are inexpensive and produce a very good shine on the finished product.

The material is, however, thin and care must be taken not to break the mould. Plastic tray moulds are also available for smaller items such as sweets. Metal moulds are much more robust but can be difficult to use. With a little ingenuity, the cost of moulds can be reduced. Tin foil cases are a useful alternative providing they are thoroughly cleaned before use.

Three-dimensional moulds are available with integral clips, or with holes, to ensure alignment and prevent seepage (see page 41).

For good results it is essential that each mould is thoroughly cleaned and polished with cotton wool or a soft cloth or tissue before use. The secret of success lies in using the chocolate at the correct temperature to ensure proper contraction of the chocolate. The form then lifts easily out of the polished mould when set. Couverture chocolate produces an infinitely superior taste for moulded forms, but compound chocolate can be used as this produces a very good finish, but lacks taste.

NOTE: *If using couverture it is necessary to temper the chocolate.*
Compound chocolate does not require tempering.

Follow steps 1-6 below to make egg and sweet moulds or chocolate cases.

TO JOIN MOULDED HALVES
Place one half face down on a warmed baking tray to slightly melt the edge. Immediately place on top of other half and align.

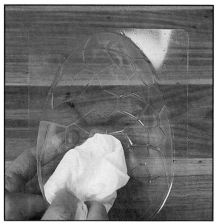

1 *To ensure easy removal of the chocolate when set, carefully polish the inside of each mould with cotton wool, soft cloth or tissue.*

2 *Melt or temper the chocolate in the usual way (see pages 8 or 9). Holding the mould horizontally, pour in the melted chocolate.*

3 *Ensure that the whole inside of the mould is covered with melted chocolate.*

4 *Immediately pour the surplus chocolate back into the bowl.*

5 *Pass a palette knife across the top of the mould to create a clean edge. Place egg moulds face down on waxed paper (sweet moulds upright) to set for approx 30 minutes.*

6 *Add another layer if necessary. Leave to set for 24 hours. Carefully ease the shape from the mould.*

Chocolate Cut-outs, Leaves and Curls

NOTE: *If using couverture, it is necessary to temper the chocolate (see page 8). If using compound chocolate, melt in the usual way (see page 9).*

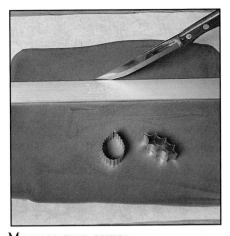

MAKING CUT-OUTS:

1 Spread the melted or tempered chocolate onto waxed paper and shake slightly to make an even surface. When nearly set, cut into shapes as required.

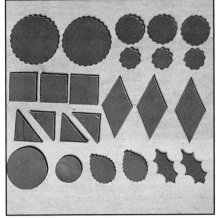

2 To ensure clean edges on each shape, press cutters firmly while cutting, without twisting. Leave to harden on greaseproof paper before using as decoration.

MAKING LEAVES:

1 Select fresh non-poisonous leaves with well-defined veins, e.g. rose or bay leaves. Leave a stem for handling. Clean with a damp cloth and dry well.

2 Using a medium-sized paint brush, thickly coat the underside of each leaf with melted chocolate. Coat up to, but not over, the edges of the leaf.

3 Place the leaves, chocolate side up, on greaseproof paper. When the chocolate is firm, carefully peel the leaf away, stem first, and leave the chocolate leaf to set.

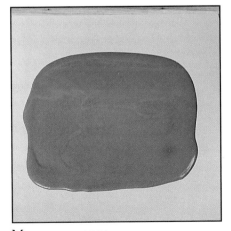

MAKING CURLS:

1 Pour melted or tempered chocolate onto a marble slab. Spread the chocolate thinly with a palette knife and leave until it is just set.

2 Holding a sharp knife at an angle of 45°, shave the surface of the chocolate to form curls. The thickness can be varied by altering the angle of the blade.

3 Place the curls on greaseproof paper and leave to set before using as decoration.

ALBUMEN SOLUTION

Ingredients:
Pure albumen powder 30g (1oz)
Water 170g (6oz)

Method:
Pour the water into a bowl. Stir the water whilst sprinkling in the dried albumen and mix thoroughly. Stir occasionally during next hour. Strain mixture through a sieve or muslin. It is then ready for use.

ROYAL ICING

Ingredients:
Fresh egg whites or albumen solution 85g (3oz)
Sieved icing sugar 455g (16oz)

Method:
Place the albumen solution or fresh egg white into a bowl. Stir in one-third of the icing sugar until dissolved. Repeat until all icing sugar is used.
Beat mixture until light and fluffy and peaks can be formed. Clean down the inside of the bowl and cover with a damp cloth until required.

SUGARPASTE

Ingredients:
Sieved icing sugar 455g (16oz)
Egg white 1
Warm glucose 60g (2oz)

Method:
Warm a bowl containing glucose in a saucepan of hot water. Place the icing sugar in a mixing bowl with the egg white. Add the warmed glucose and mix thoroughly. Knead the mixture to a pliable paste before wrapping in a polythene bag. Store in a cool place.

Sugarpaste can be coloured or flavoured, and used as a covering for cakes or as a chocolate centre. It is firm and sweet and is generally used for covering cakes by rolling it out into sheet form, in a similar manner to marzipan/almond paste.

BUTTERCREAM

Ingredients:
Butter 170g (6oz)
Sieved icing sugar 340g (12oz)
Warm water 3 tablespoons

Method:
Soften the butter and beat until light. Gradually add the icing sugar, beating well after each addition. Beat in the water. Add colour and flavour as required.

CHOCOLATE BUTTERCREAM

Ingredients:
Buttercream 225g (8oz)
Melted compound or couverture chocolate 60g (2oz)

Method:
Melt the compound or couverture to 38°C (100°F) and immediately beat into the buttercream.

ALMOND PASTE

Ingredients:
Caster sugar 170g (6oz)
Sieved icing sugar 170g (6oz)
Ground almonds 340g (12oz)
Glucose syrup 225g (8oz)

Method:
Mix together the dry ingredients. Warm and pour in the glucose (the consistency of the paste can be altered by adjusting the amount of glucose).
Mix together to form a pliable paste and store in a sealed container until required.

FLOWER PASTE

Ingredients:
Cornflour 60g (2oz)
Icing sugar 400g (14oz)
Gum tragacanth 22g (¾oz)
Glucose syrup 22g (¾oz)
Cold water 60g (2oz)
White fat 22g (¾oz)

Method:
Weigh all the ingredients carefully. Place the dry ingredients onto greaseproof paper and sieve three times into a bowl. Add the remaining ingredients and mix thoroughly on a 'slow' machine, or by hand with a wooden spoon. When paste is mixed properly it should not stick to the sides of the bowl. Mould the paste into a ball and place in a polythene bag. Leave to mature for at least 24 hours before use.

NOTE: Instructions and ideas for making sugar flowers to decorate Easter eggs and cakes are contained in the Mary Ford book *Sugar Flowers Cake Decorating*.

Hints And Tips

○ **Storing** — Chocolate should be stored in a cool dry place, preferably at 10°C (50°F). Do not store chocolate in the refrigerator.

— As chocolate easily absorbs strong odours, opened blocks, buttons or grated chocolate should be sealed in waxed paper before storing.

○ **Melting** — Melt chocolate slowly on a very low heat, stirring gently.

— Never try to hurry the melting process by turning up the heat.

— Do not cover chocolate whilst being melted, or chocolate which is melted.

— Buttons, or chocolate which has been grated or cut into small pieces, will melt more quickly and easily than block chocolate.

— Melted chocolate should be stirred slowly when directed, not beaten, as this forms bubbles.

— If melted chocolate is too thick, thin it with a small amount of lard. Never add water as this causes chocolate to stiffen.

○ **Tempering** — It is essential to use the temperatures specified for milk or plain couverture for correct results. Couverture can also be cooled on a marble slab during the tempering process.

○ **Coating** — Chocolate compound is better for coating cakes as it cuts more easily than couverture chocolate.

○ **Couverture** — Couverture has a superior taste to that of chocolate compound and is thoroughly recommended for all confections in this book.

— Couverture requires tempering unless otherwise specified. Always read the note regarding tempering at the start of each recipe or confection being made.

○ **Grating** — Before grating chocolate, place the wrapped chocolate block in the refrigerator for an hour to chill.

— When grating chocolate, use a coarse grater.

— Grated chocolate makes a quick and attractive topping for desserts and ice-cream and is a useful coating for cakes.

— Grated chocolate can be used in place of vermicelli.

○ **Chocolate Shavings** — When making chocolate shavings, allow the block to reach 27°C (80°F) in a warm room and then finely 'shave' the chocolate with a potato peeler. Use long smooth strokes to achieve a quick curl.

○ **Moulds** — Moulds must be clean, dry and polished thoroughly before use.

— Do not use abrasive materials to clean moulds as these will scratch the surface.

— It is inadvisable to use a scratched mould.

— Always cover the entire inside surface of the mould with chocolate.

— Rubber bands or paper clips can be used to hold moulds together when making three-dimensional shapes.

○ **Piping** — Stir glycerol slowly into the chocolate as otherwise the chocolate can become too thick if too much glycerol is added.

— Piping chocolate can be made by mixing a few drops of water with melted chocolate.

—Keep piping chocolate warm, but not hot, whilst in use, by standing basin over hot water.

— Use small or medium sized piping bags for decorating chocolate confectionery.

○ **General** — Keep chocolate away from direct sunlight as much as possible.

— Work in a cool room 18°C (65°F) when using chocolate.

— Do not allow water to come into contact with chocolate (unless specified in the recipe) and ensure that all utensils are absolutely dry.

— When handling chocolate or sweets, wear disposable plastic gloves.

○ **Cocoa** — Cocoa powder is the most economical chocolate flavouring for use in cooking. Cocoa powder should be sieved with the dry ingredients where possible.

○ **Colouring white chocolate** — White chocolate can be coloured using confectioners' dusting powder or special oil-based colouring. A very small amount of colour should be thoroughly worked into the melted chocolate until the desired colour is achieved.

Bitter Orange

INGREDIENTS

Milk couverture or compound chocolate 455g (16oz)
Minced orange peel 340g (12oz)
Honey 225g (8oz)
Chocolate hazelnut spread 115g (4oz)
Orange zest 22g (¾oz)

Note: If using couverture in this recipe, it is not necessary to temper the chocolate.

Dipping:
Plain couverture or compound chocolate 340g (12oz)

Note: If using couverture for dipping, the chocolate must be tempered (see page 8). If using compound chocolate, this must be melted in the usual way (see page 9).

Decoration:
Milk piping chocolate (see page 55)
Crystallised orange

ITEMS REQUIRED
Baking tray 29cm x 19cm (11½″ x 7½″)
Silicone paper
Greaseproof paper
Small round cutters
Waxed paper
Piping bags
Piping tube No.42

Makes approximately 80 sweets
Eat within 3 months

1 Melt the chocolate in the usual way (see page 9). Warm the honey in a separate bowl. Mix the peel and the hazelnut spread into the melted chocolate.

2 Sprinkle on the orange zest then pour in the warmed honey. Mix together well.

3 Line the base of a baking tray with silicone paper and pour in the mixture. Rough up the surface with a fork and leave to set for 24 hours.

4 Remove from tin and cut some of the mixture into small, narrow sticks. Place the sticks onto greaseproof paper and leave to dry for 2 hours.

5 Cut the remaining mixture into long strips. Using a small round cutter, cut each strip into crescent shapes. Leave to dry for 2 hours.

6 Melt or temper the chocolate for dipping. Dip each stick into the chocolate and leave to set on waxed paper in a cool place for 2 hours.

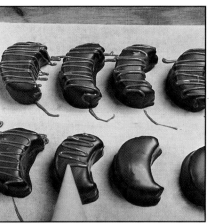

7 Dip a third of the crescent shapes into the prepared chocolate. Decorate with a tiny piece of crystallised orange.

8 Dip another third of the pieces and leave to set. Decorate with piping chocolate (see page 55), as shown.

9 Decorate the remaining crescents with piped lines of melted chocolate.

Nut Crunch

Ingredients

Water 60g (2oz)
Granulated sugar 455g (16oz)
Flaked almonds – (lightly roasted and chopped) 85g (3oz)
Milk couverture or compound chocolate 455g (16oz)
Chocolate hazelnut spread 170g (6oz)

Note: If using couverture in this recipe, it is not necessary to temper the chocolate.

Dipping:
Plain couverture or compound chocolate 340g (12oz)

Note: If using couverture for dipping, the chocolate must be tempered (see page 8). If using compound chocolate, this must be melted in the usual way (see page 9).

Items Required

Silicone paper
Swiss roll tin 29cm x 19cm (11½″ x 7½″) lined with
   silicone paper
Rolling pin
Palette knife
Piping bag

Makes approximately 80 sweets
Eat within 3 months

1 Pour the water into a saucepan and add the sugar. Heat gently until a golden brown toffee is reached. Remove from heat.

2 Immediately add the chopped nuts and stir with a wooden spoon until evenly mixed.

3 Carefully pour the toffee mixture onto silicone paper.

4 Using a palette knife, immediately spread the toffee as thinly as possible and leave until cold.

5 Remove the toffee from the silicone and break into small pieces. Place in a bowl and crunch the pieces with a rolling pin, or mince.

6 The toffee should be finely ground to resemble coarse breadcrumbs.

7 Melt the chocolate in the usual way (see page 9). Stir in the hazelnut spread and the crunched toffee.

8 Pour the mixture into the lined swiss roll tin and spread with a palette knife. Leave to set for 24 hours.

9 Turn out, mark and cut into squares. Dip into melted or tempered chocolate and decorate the tops with a variety of finishes.

Making Fondant

INGREDIENTS

Cube sugar 905g (2lbs)
Water 285g (10oz)
Glucose, warmed 170g (6oz)

ITEMS REQUIRED

Marble slab
Metal bars
Sugar thermometer
2 palette knives

Fondant can also be purchased in powdered form and
mixed to the right consistency by adding water.

1 Oil the marble slab and bars lightly,
using an area 45.5cm x 45.5cm (18"
x 18") for each 905g (2lbs) of sugar.

2 To prepare the fondant, place the
sugar cubes and water into a saucepan
and heat until the sugar dissolves. DO
NOT BOIL.

3 When 107°C (225°F) is reached,
pour in the warmed glucose and bring
to the boil. DO NOT STIR.

4 Whilst mixture is still boiling, lightly
brush water on the inside of the
saucepan to prevent crystals forming.

5 Continue to fast boil until a temperature of 116°C (240°F) is reached to
give a clear syrup.

6 At 116°C (240°F), remove syrup
from the heat and place it in a bowl of
cold water for 2 minutes.

7 Form a rectangle on the marble slab placing the bars on the oiled area. Pour the syrup onto the slab between the bars. DO NOT SCRAPE OUT THE SAUCEPAN.

8 Leave the syrup to cool until it reaches a temperature of 38°C (100°F).

9 When cooled to 38°C (100°F), remove bars. Using a palette knife, start to turn the syrup by repeatedly taking the outside edges to centre.

10 The syrup will thicken to a white mass. Continue mixing until the fondant is cold. It will be necessary to use a palette knife in each hand.

11 Cover the fondant with a damp cloth and leave for 30 minutes.

12 Mix the fondant for another 5 minutes before transferring it to a sealed container. Store in a cool place until required.

This fondant can be used for making chocolate covered fondants or fondant centres (see page 21).

This fondant can also be used for covering gateaux (see page 77).

This fondant can also be used for topping (see page 91).

Fondants

INGREDIENTS

Fondant 455g (16oz)
Food colouring and flavouring of choice

Moulds and Dipping:
Plain couverture or compound chocolate 340g (12oz)

Note: If using couverture for dipping, the chocolate must be tempered (see page 8). If using compound chocolate, this must be melted in the usual way (see page 9).

ITEMS REQUIRED

Cornflour
Baking trays 4cm (1½") deep
Heavy based saucepan
Sugar thermometer
Piping bag
Greaseproof paper
Pastry brush
Chocolate moulds
Dipping fork

Makes approximately 30 sweets
Eat within 3 months

1 Warm the cornflour slightly then sieve it into the baking tray.

2 Level the top of the cornflour with a smooth-sided ruler or straight edge. Ensure there is sufficient cornflour to fill the tray completely.

3 Using a dowel or chocolate mould, make impressions in the cornflour to form moulds. Approximately 30 moulds are required.

4 Heat the fondant to 60°C (140°F) and then add a few drops of colour and flavour of choice.

5 Fill a piping bag with the warm fondant and quickly pipe into each of the moulds.

6 After 3 hours, remove the fondants and place on greaseproof paper. Leave to harden for 24 hours. Then brush lightly to remove any excess cornflour.

7 Picture shows fondant shapes made from patterned cornflour moulds.

8 For covered fondants, pipe melted chocolate into a chocolate mould, drop in a fondant and seal with more chocolate. Leave for 24 hours. Remove from mould.

9 For half-dipped fondants, dip into melted or tempered chocolate, using a dipping fork.

Turkish Delight

INGREDIENTS

Gelatine 30g (1oz)
Water 145g (5oz)
Granulated sugar 455g (16oz)
Water 145g (5oz)
Honey 60g (2oz)
Essence or flavouring of choice
Edible food colouring

Dusting:
Cornflour 30g (1oz)
Icing sugar 30g (1oz)

Dipping:
Plain couverture or compound chocolate 340g (12oz)

Note: If using couverture for dipping, the chocolate must be tempered (see page 8). If using compound chocolate, this must be melted in the usual way (see page 9).

ITEMS REQUIRED

Sugar thermometer
Whisk
Baking tray 20.5cm x 13cm (8″ x 5″)
Greaseproof paper

Makes approximately 50 sweets
Eat within 6 months

Storage:
If not covered with chocolate, Turkish Delight should be sprinkled with dusting mixture and must be stored in an airtight container lined with greaseproof paper.

1 *Sprinkle the gelatine into 145g (5oz) of water and leave to dissolve for approximately 5 minutes.*

2 *Boil the sugar with 145g (5oz) of water. DO NOT STIR. At 107°C (225°F) remove from heat and stir in the honey. Return to heat and boil to 118°C (245°F).*

3 *Remove mixture from heat and pour it into the dissolved gelatine, stirring well. Add colour and flavouring of choice.*

4 *Pour the mixture into a water-splashed tray and leave to set in a cool place for 24 hours.*

5 *Mix the cornflour and icing sugar together and sprinkle onto the surface of the set Turkish Delight. Also dust a sheet of greaseproof paper.*

6 *Remove the Turkish Delight from the tin by gently pulling and rolling it up. Place onto the dusted greaseproof paper.*

7 Cut the Turkish Delight into neat squares and place into dusting mixture to cover completely.

8 Place the pieces onto a baking tray and leave to dry for 24 hours.

9 Remove surplus dusting mixture by shaking the pieces in a sieve. Dip half the pieces with melted or tempered chocolate (see pages 8 or 9) and leave to set.

Nut Fudge

Ingredients

Plain couverture or compound chocolate 455g (16oz)
Condensed milk 400g (14oz)
Vanilla essence 1 teaspoon
Chopped walnuts 60g (2oz)

Note: If using couverture in this recipe, it is not necessary to temper the chocolate.

Dipping:

Plain couverture or compound chocolate 340g (12oz)

Note: If using couverture for dipping, the chocolate must be tempered (see page 8). If using compound chocolate, this must be melted in the usual way (see page 9).

Decoration:

Milk piping chocolate (see page 55)

Items Required

Baking tray 29cm x 19cm (11½" x 7½") lightly greased with butter
Greaseproof paper
Waxed paper

Makes approximately 10 fudge bars and 48 chocolate diamonds
Eat within 3 months

1 Place the chocolate in a heat-proof bowl and melt in the usual way (see page 9).

2 Using a wooden spoon, stir the condensed milk and vanilla essence into the melted chocolate.

3 Mix the chopped walnuts into the chocolate mixture until an even fudge texture is formed.

4 Spread the fudge into the greased baking tray and leave to set for 24 hours in a cool dry place.

5 Turn out onto greaseproof paper and cut the fudge into bars and diamonds.

6 Melt or temper the chocolate for dipping (see pages 8 or 9). Using a dipping fork, dip each piece and place onto waxed paper to set.

7 Fill a bag with melted milk chocolate and pipe the design shown onto each bar shape.

8 Pipe the design shown on half the diamond-shaped pieces and leave to set.

9 Pipe the design shown on the remaining diamond-shaped pieces and leave to set.

Liqueur Chocolates

1 *Boil the sugar and water until the syrup reaches 107°C (225°F). Use a wet brush to wash away any crystals forming around the inside of the pan while boiling.*

2 *Pour the hot syrup into the jars and immediately seal each one to prevent crystallisation.*

3 *Taking one jar at a time, quickly unscrew the lid and pour in one of the liqueurs. Shake gently to let out the air and re-seal immediately.*

4 *Turn the sealed jars gently to mix the liqueur and syrup. Cool the jars, first in tepid water, then in cold running water. Leave for 24 hours.*

5 *Make approximately 30 chocolate moulds (see page 10), using tempered or melted chocolate. Place on a level surface ready to pour in the liqueur.*

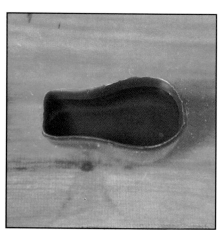

6 *Carefully fill each mould with liqueur syrup to within 0.3cm (⅛") of the top.*

7 Leave the liqueurs for at least 24 hours, or until a firm sugar coating has formed on the surface.

8 Melt or temper the chocolate in the usual way (see pages 8 or 9). Fill a piping bag and carefully pipe into each mould.

9 Gently pass a palette knife over the top of each liqueur to seal, and leave to set in a cool, dry place for 1 hour. Then remove from moulds.

Rum Truffles

INGREDIENTS

Milk couverture or compound chocolate 455g (16oz)
Milk 145g (5oz)
Rum (or flavouring of choice*) 2 teaspoons
* Brandy, orange, milk, vanilla or honey.

Note: If using couverture in this recipe, it is not necessary to temper the chocolate.

Dipping:
Milk chocolate 115g (4oz)

Note: If using couverture for dipping, the chocolate must be tempered (see page 8) OR, if using compound chocolate, this must be melted in the usual way (see page 9).

Covering:
Sieved icing sugar 115g (4oz)

ITEMS REQUIRED

Savoy piping bag
Savoy tube 0.6cm (¼") diameter
Waxed paper

Makes approximately 30 truffles
Eat within 10 days

1 Place the chocolate in a heat-proof bowl and melt in the usual way (see page 9).

2 Boil the milk and immediately pour it into the melted chocolate, stirring continuously.

3 Pour in the rum (or flavouring of choice) and stir into the mixture.

4 Continue stirring the mixture quickly to avoid lumps developing.

5 Stir the mixture, which will thicken as it cools, until a smooth creamy truffle is formed.

6 Pipe the truffle mixture onto waxed paper using the savoy piping bag and tube.

7 Flatten the tops of the truffles with the back of a spoon and leave to set for 1 hour. Melt or temper the chocolate for dipping (see page 8 or 9).

8 Sieve the icing sugar into a bowl. Using a fork, dip a truffle into the chocolate.

9 Immediately place it into the icing sugar. With a second fork, immediately roll the truffle until completely covered. Dip and cover each truffle separately.

Mint Crisps

INGREDIENTS

Plain couverture or compound chocolate 225g (8oz)
Brown sugar 115g (4oz)
Peppermint oil 2 teaspoons

Note: If using couverture, the chocolate must be tempered (see page 8) OR, if using compound chocolate, this must be melted in the usual way (see page 9).

ALTERNATIVE FLAVOURINGS

Prepare any one of the following fillings and mix into the melted or tempered chocolate and brown sugar.

○ **Orange:** Add the grated rind of 1 medium sized orange.

○ **Coffee:** Mix 1 teaspoon of coffee powder with a few drops of water to form a stiff paste, then add to the chocolate and sugar.

○ **Ginger:** Add 2 tablespoons of chopped preserved ginger.

ITEMS REQUIRED

Greaseproof paper
Trowel-shaped palette knife
Crimp-shaped cutter
Shallow moulds

Makes approximately 50 crisps
Eat within 3 months

1 Place the chocolate in a heat-proof bowl and melt or temper in the usual way (see pages 8 or 9).

2 Pour in the brown sugar and stir until it is evenly dispersed.

3 Add the peppermint oil and stir in thoroughly.

4 Cool the mixture slightly by placing the bowl into cold water, stirring occasionally, then remove from the cold water.

5 Spread half the mixture onto grease-proof paper, using a trowel-shaped palette knife. Leave until almost set.

6 Cut out shapes with a crimp-shaped cutter and place onto a separate sheet of greaseproof paper. Leave to set.

7 Spread the remaining mixture onto greaseproof paper and, when almost set, cut along a straight edge with a sharp knife to form parallel strips.

8 Cut each strip into small oblongs and place onto a separate sheet of greaseproof paper to set.

9 Re-melt the scraps of chocolate and spoon into shallow moulds. Leave to harden. Remove from moulds and store all crisps in a box until required.

Walnut and Almond

INGREDIENTS

Almond paste 455g (16oz)
Chopped walnuts 85g (3oz)

Dipping:
Milk couverture or compound chocolate 455g (16oz)
Walnut halves 60g (2oz)
Chopped walnuts 115g (4oz)

Note: If using couverture for dipping, the chocolate must be tempered (see page 8). If using compound chocolate, this must be melted in the usual way (see page 9).

ITEMS REQUIRED

Greaseproof paper
Two-pronged dipping fork
Waxed paper
Rolling pin
Ring-shaped dipping fork

Makes approximately 60 sweets
Eat within 6 months

1 Thoroughly mix the chopped walnuts into the almond paste until evenly dispersed.

2 Carefully cut and shape the paste into small oblongs, flat rounds and ball-shaped pieces. Leave to dry for 2 hours on greaseproof paper.

3 Melt or temper the chocolate in the usual way (see pages 8 or 9). Using a dipping fork, dip an oblong piece into the melted chocolate.

4 Immediately place the oblong onto waxed paper and carefully remove the fork.

5 Place half a walnut on top whilst the chocolate is still wet. Continue dipping and topping each oblong and leave to set.

6 Dip each round piece, marking the tops with a two-pronged dipping fork. Leave to set.

7 Crush some walnuts on greaseproof paper, using a rolling pin. Place the crushed walnuts into a small bowl.

8 Using a ring-shaped dipping fork, dip a ball into the chocolate, then drop it into the chopped walnuts.

9 Immediately roll the ball around until it is completely coated. Repeat with remaining balls, one at a time. Leave to set.

Coconut Ice

INGREDIENTS

Milk 145g (5oz)
Granulated sugar 455g (16oz)
Desiccated coconut 145g (5oz)
Vanilla essence 2 drops
Edible food colouring

Dipping:
Plain couverture or compound chocolate 340g (12oz)

Note: If using couverture for dipping, the chocolate must be tempered (see page 8). If using compound chocolate, this must be melted in the usual way (see page 9).

Decoration:
Toasted coconut

ITEMS REQUIRED

Lightly greased tray 29cm x 19cm (11½″ x 7½″)
Palette knife
Serrated knife
Waxed paper

Makes approximately 12 bars and 60 sweets
Eat within 6 months

1 *Pour the milk into a saucepan and add the sugar. Dissolve slowly over a low heat and boil steadily for 10 minutes. Remove from heat.*

2 *When the bubbles have subsided, stir in the coconut and vanilla essence.*

3 *Using a palette knife, spread half the mixture into the lightly greased tray.*

4 *Colour the remaining half of the mixture with edible food colouring and pour on top of the white layer.*

5 *Immediately smooth out the mixture to the sides of the tray, completely covering the white layer. Leave to set for 24 hours.*

6 *Carefully turn out the coconut ice. Using a sharp pointed knife and straight edge, mark it into large and small bars.*

7 Following the marked lines, cut the coconut ice with a serrated knife. Leave to set for 2 hours.

8 Carefully dip a corner of each large bar into melted or tempered chocolate (see pages 8 or 9). Place on waxed paper to set.

9 Completely dip each small bar and place onto waxed paper. Whilst still wet, sprinkle toasted coconut on top to decorate and leave to set.

Fruit Liqueurs

INGREDIENTS

Plain couverture or compound chocolate 570g (1¼lb)
Fondant 100g (4oz)
Kirsch or other liqueur
Selection of best quality fresh fruits, cleaned and dried

Note: If using couverture, the chocolate must be tempered (see page 8). If using compound chocolate, this must be melted in the usual way (see page 9).

ITEMS REQUIRED

Chocolate moulds
Sieve
Piping bag

Makes approximately 50 sweets
Eat within 10 days

1 Melt or temper the chocolate in the usual way (see pages 8 or 9) and make 50 moulds (see page 10). Leave to set for 1 hour.

2 Cover each shape with a second layer of chocolate. Leave to set for one hour.

3 Cut the different fruits into small pieces and leave to soak in the liqueur overnight.

4 Drain the fruits separately by pouring them into a sieve. Keep to one side until needed.

5 Warm the fondant to approximately 38°C (100°F) and stir in Kirsch, or other liqueur, to taste.

6 Fill a piping bag and pipe a small bulb of fondant into each of the chocolate moulds.

7 Top each of the fondant-filled chocolate cases with the prepared fruits.

8 Fill a piping bag with melted or tempered chocolate and fill each of the moulds, covering the fruit completely. Leave to set for 20 minutes.

9 Pipe in a second layer of chocolate to bring the surface level with the top of each mould. Leave to set for 24 hours, then remove from the moulds.

Chocolate Cream Cups

INGREDIENTS

Cases:

Plain couverture or compound chocolate 455g (16oz)

Note: If using couverture for moulds, the chocolate must be tempered (see page 8) OR, if using compound chocolate, this must be melted in the usual way (see page 9).

Filling:

White couverture or compound chocolate 340g (12oz)
Milk 145g (5oz)
Caster sugar 30g (1oz)
Liqueur of choice

Note: If using couverture in the filling, it is not necessary to temper the chocolate.

ITEMS REQUIRED

Fluted chocolate moulds
Plaque mould
Piping bags
Star savoy tube

Makes approximately 50 Cream Cups
Eat within 2 months

1 *Melt or temper the chocolate (see pages 8 or 9) and make 50 fluted chocolate cases (see page 10).*

MAKING THE FILLING:

2 *Melt the white chocolate in the usual way (see page 8). Pour the milk into a separate saucepan and add the sugar. Bring to the boil.*

3 *Pour the hot milk and sugar onto the melted chocolate.*

4 *Immediately stir the mixture, then beat well until smooth.*

5 *Add the liqueur to the mixture and leave to cool.*

6 *When the mixture is cool, whisk until a light cream is formed.*

7 Pipe the cream into the fluted chocolate cases and leave to set for 2 hours. Store in the refrigerator until required.

8 To make a plaque, fill the head shape of an appropriate mould with melted or tempered white chocolate and leave to set.

9 Then complete the mould, covering the head with tempered or melted milk chocolate. Leave to set.

Almond Clusters

1 *Temper 225g (8oz) of couverture (see page 8), or melt compound chocolate in the usual way (see page 9). Stir in 115g (4oz) of roasted nib almonds.*

2 *Thoroughly mix the almonds into the chocolate until evenly dispersed.*

3 *Immediately place spoonfuls of the mixture onto waxed paper and into paper sweet cases. Leave to set for 2 hours. Eat within 6 months.*

Chocolate Hen

Couverture or compound chocolate 455g (16oz)

Note: If using couverture, the chocolate must be tempered (see page 8). If using compound chocolate, this must be melted in the usual way (see page 9).

ITEMS REQUIRED

Cotton wool
Hen mould
Wire tray
Basket
Foil-wrapped chocolate eggs
Shredded glacine paper

1 Melt or temper, in the usual way, sufficient chocolate for the mould (see pages 8 or 9).

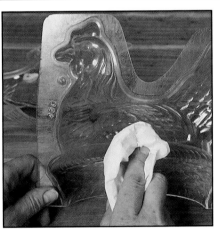

2 Wash the moulds in warm water and dry thoroughly. Polish the insides with cotton wool, soft cloth or tissue to ensure easy removal of the chocolate.

3 Clip the 2 halves of the mould together and pour in the melted chocolate. Turn the mould to allow the chocolate to cover the entire inside surface.

4 Pour the surplus chocolate back into the bowl and stand the mould upright on a wire tray to drain. Leave until just set.

5 To increase the thickness of the chocolate, add another layer by repeating steps 3-4.

6 When completely set, carefully dismantle the mould to release the chocolate moulded hen.

Filled Easter Eggs

1 Make as many half eggs and bases as required using tempered couverture or melted compound chocolate (see page 10).

2 Fill a half egg with shredded glacine paper then with assorted sweets and chocolates.

3 Place a half egg of the same size onto a warmed baking tray to slightly melt the edge.

4 Immediately place onto the filled egg and align. Leave to set for 10 minutes on a suitable surface, to prevent it rolling around.

5 To decorate, pipe tiny shells of melted chocolate around the edges to conceal the join.

6 When the decoration is dry, wrap the egg in foil and tie with ribbon.

7 Alternatively, fix the egg to a chocolate base, supporting it while it sets.

8 Fill a piping bag with coloured royal icing and pipe rosettes around the join (No.7).

9 Cut out marzipan shapes to make a design and complete the decoration by piping an Easter message with royal icing.

10 *Designs can be varied to suit the individual members of a family.*

11 *This example with flowers and rabbit motif would also be suitable for a young child.*

12 *Other designs can be created to suit the individual's hobby or favourite sport.*

Decorated Easter Egg

1 Make 2 chocolate egg halves (see page 10) and fix together. Make a chocolate basket for the base.

2 Pipe a decorative border with piping chocolate (see page 55) around the edge to conceal the join (No. 43).

3 Sit the egg inside a chocolate basket with some shredded glacine paper. Decorate with flowers and motif, as shown.

Decorated Half Egg

1 Make half a chocolate egg (see page 10) and fix it upright on a chocolate base.

2 Pipe scrolls of piping chocolate (see page 55) onto waxed paper and leave to set (No. 43). Then fix the scrolls to the edges as shown.

3 Decorate the inside of the egg with sugar flowers, leaves and grass. Add an Easter chick to complete the decoration.

Large Decorated Easter Egg

ITEMS REQUIRED

Large chocolate egg (see page 10)
Chocolate base
Round cake board
Savoy piping bag
Piping tube No's. 44, 2 & 1

Decoration:

Royal icing
Spray of silk flowers
Chicks

1 Prepare a whole chocolate egg (see page 10) and mount it securely on a base.

2 For easy handling, stand the egg and base on a cake board. Pipe shells of royal icing around the edge to conceal join (No. 44).

3 Pipe a rope design in scallops beside, and over, the large shells (No. 2).

4 Pipe spikes on the central rope line (No. 1).

5 Pipe decorative tracery and dots onto the chocolate egg (No. 1), as shown.

6 Fix silk flowers and ribbon to the sides of the chocolate egg to form a spray.

7 Pipe an inscription of choice in the style shown (No. 2).

8 Overpipe the inscription (No. 1) and then decorate with tracery and small shells.

9 Fix the chicks, and appropriate message with ribbon, to the egg and base.

Chick Easter Egg

1 Starting with its centre, press coloured almond paste into the flower and leaves at the base of the egg.

2 Next, fill the walking stick, beak, feet and bow tie with appropriately coloured almond paste.

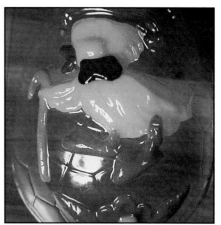

3 Fill the body and head of the chick by pressing the yellow almond paste in a little at a time.

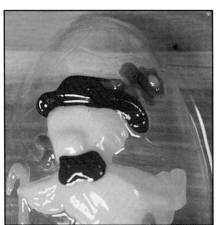

4 Fill the flower above the chick, in the same way as the first flower.

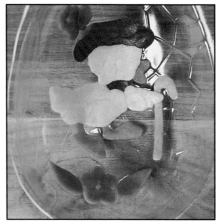

5 Picture shows the inside of the egg. Leave to dry for 2 hours.

6 Melt or temper the chocolate in the usual way (see pages 8 or 9) and pour into the mould to cover the whole of the inside.

7 Drain the surplus chocolate from the mould back into the bowl and keep warm for making the second half of the egg.

8 Place the mould face down onto waxed paper.

9 Make a second shell, without the chick. Leave to set for 24 hours. Remove from moulds and fix together. Then mount on a base and decorate as shown.

Chocolate Cream Eggs

INGREDIENTS

Moulds:
Couverture or compound chocolate 225g (8oz)

Filling:
Sieved icing sugar 455g (16oz)
Gelatine 30g (1oz)
Water 115g (4oz)
Egg white 200g (7oz)

Note: If using couverture, the chocolate must be tempered (see page 8). If using compound chocolate, this must be melted in the usual way (see page 9).

ITEMS REQUIRED

Chocolate moulds (hen egg size)
Piping bag
Palette knife
Silver foil or coloured sweet foils

Eat within 7 days

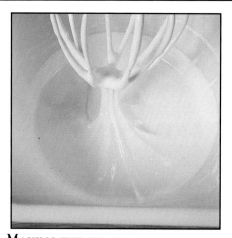

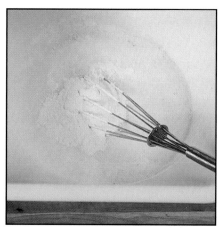

1 Make 20 egg halves with melted or tempered chocolate (see page 10).

MAKING THE FILLING:
2 Warm the icing sugar until hand hot. Dissolve the gelatine in the water. Pour the egg white into a grease-free bowl and whisk until stiff.

3 Add the warmed icing sugar to the egg white and mix thoroughly until cold.

4 Mix the dissolved gelatine into the egg white and icing sugar.

5 Immediately pipe the cream filling into the chocolate eggs to within 0.3cm (⅛") of the top, taking care not to spill any over the sides.

6 Leave the filled eggs in a cool place until a skin has formed over the filling.

7 Pipe melted chocolate over the cream filling until level with the top of each egg.

8 Pass a palette knife over the surface of each egg to seal the filling completely. Leave to set for approximately 15 minutes.

9 Gently tap the eggs out of the mould, chilling beforehand if necessary. Place 2 halves together and wrap in silver foil or coloured sweet foils.

Crinoline Lady

1 Make a whole chocolate egg (see page 10). Cut off one end and place onto a base. Fix a figure on the top, as shown.

2 Mould chocolate paste (see page 67) into 'petal' shapes and build up over the egg to form the skirt.

3 Fix a spray of silk flowers to the skirt, together with small bows of ribbon around the hem. Cut a heart shape from chocolate and pipe with an Easter message.

Cracked Easter Egg

1 Make a whole chocolate egg (see page 10) and lay it on its side on soft paper.

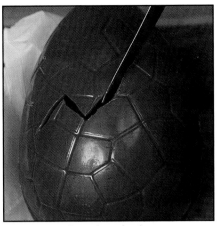

2 Using a hot, sharp knife, cut zigzags around the middle of the egg to simulate a cracked egg.

3 Fix the two halves onto a base. Fill with assorted, wrapped sweets and shredded glacine paper. Decorate with chick and bow of ribbon.

Novelty Egg

1 Make a whole chocolate egg (see page 10) and fix it in an upright position onto a base, using a little melted chocolate.

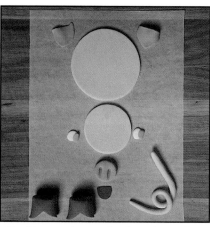

2 Cut out shapes of coloured marzipan or sugarpaste, as shown. Place on greaseproof paper and leave to dry for 24 hours.

3 Pipe shells of piping chocolate (see page 55) around the egg to conceal the join. Fix the marzipan shapes onto the egg, as shown, using melted chocolate.

Making Piping Chocolate

INGREDIENTS

Couverture or compound chocolate
225g (8oz)
Glycerol approximately ½ teaspoon

Note: If using couverture, it is
necessary to temper the
chocolate. Compound chocolate
does not require tempering.

1   *Place the chocolate in a heat-proof
bowl and melt or temper in the usual
way (see pages 8 or 9).*

2   *Remove the chocolate from the heat.
Add the glycerol and stir immediately.*

3   *Continue stirring and adding glycerol
until the required consistency is
reached. Keep the mixture warm, and use
before it sets.*

Filigree Egg

Piping chocolate:
115gm (4oz) of piping chocolate (see page 55) will be sufficient for a 15cm (6″) high egg mould.

Note: If using couverture for the egg, the chocolate must be tempered (see page 8) OR, if using compound chocolate, this must be melted in the usual way (see page 9).

Decoration:
Sugar flowers
Bows and ribbon loops

ITEMS REQUIRED

Easter egg mould
Piping bag
Piping tube No. 7
Palette knife
Waxed paper
Chocolate base

1 Prepare the piping chocolate (see page 55), taking care not to add too much glycerol. Keep the chocolate warm.

2 Fill a piping bag with the prepared piping chocolate.

3 Pipe on the inside of the mould with the piping chocolate, covering the sides completely, using a rotating movement to create the open effect.

4 Pass the palette knife across the top of the mould to level the edges.

5 Place the mould face down onto waxed paper and leave in a cool place for approximately 2 hours or until set. Then carefully remove from the mould.

6 Repeat steps 2-5 to make the other half of the egg. Join together with a little melted chocolate and fix to the chocolate base.

7 Fill a bag with piping chocolate and pipe shells along the edge to conceal join (No. 7).

8 Decorate the outside of the filigree egg with different coloured sugar flowers and ribbon loops.

9 Complete the decoration by fixing bows of coloured ribbon around the egg and base.

Egg House

Decoration:
Royal icing 115g (4oz)
Edible food colouring
Ribbon
Chicks

ITEMS REQUIRED
Greaseproof paper
2 egg halves 15cm (6") high (see page 10)
1 base 13cm (5") diameter
2 chocolate oblongs 15cm x 7.5cm (6" x 3") (see page 11)
1 chocolate oblong 10cm x 4cm (4" x 1½")
Waxed paper
Templates
Piping bag
Piping tube No.43
Round cutter 4cm (1½") diameter
Square cake board 20.5cm (8")

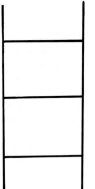

1 Lay out all the chocolate pieces on a sheet of greaseproof paper (see pages 10 and 11).

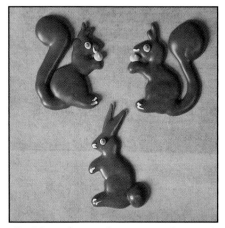

2 Using the templates as a guide, pipe 2 squirrels and 8 rabbits onto waxed paper with melted or tempered chocolate. Decorate with coloured icing.

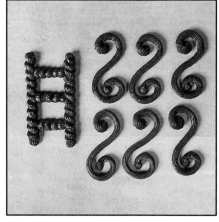

3 Fill a bag with piping chocolate (see page 55) and pipe 6 scrolls and a ladder (No. 43) onto waxed paper using templates as a guide.

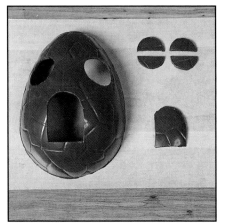

4 Warm the round cutter and carefully cut holes for windows. Using a hot knife, cut out a door. Cut the window pieces in half, as shown, to form sills.

5 Join the half eggs together and fix in an upright position on the chocolate base.

6 Pipe royal icing shells (No. 43) around egg join. Cut 2 semi-circles from the ends of the roof sides and fix to egg as shown. Fix and decorate roof.

7 Attach the window sills, door and roof platform, as shown. Then fix the 6 piped scrolls to the roof sides.

8 Pipe royal icing shells around remaining edges. Fix the house to a cake board, then stipple the board with royal icing to give a grass effect.

9 Complete the house by fixing the ladder and adding chocolate rabbits around its base and squirrels on the roof. Flowers and chicks can be positioned as shown.

Easter Rabbit

Rabbit:
Plain couverture or compound chocolate

Decoration:
Royal icing

Note: If using couverture, the chocolate must be tempered (see page 8). If using compound chocolate, this must be melted in the usual way (see page 9).

see page 8
see page 9

ITEMS REQUIRED
Rabbit mould
Piping bag
Ribbon
Sugar flowers and leaves
Cake board
Sugarpaste

1 Make a chocolate rabbit (see page 41), and fix it onto the board using a little melted chocolate.

see page 41

2 Stipple the board with royal icing and pipe around the base to simulate grass.

3 Cut out and fix shapes of sugarpaste for the inner ears and eyes.

4 Cut out and fix a sugarpaste nose. Pipe royal icing whiskers as shown.

5 Make and fix a sugarpaste bow tie, shirt cuffs and watch. Pipe small dots on the bow tie with royal icing.

6 Arrange and fix flowers, leaves, ribbon and chick to complete the basket.

7 Make and fix sugarpaste trouser cuffs, knee patch and pocket. Then decorate the pocket and knee patch with royal icing, as shown.

8 Fix further sugar flowers in the grass around the base of the rabbit.

9 Pipe an Easter message onto a chocolate disc and fix to the base. Add chicks to complete the decoration of the board.

Chocolate and Coffee Flake Sponge

INGREDIENTS

Melted butter 60g (2oz)
Caster sugar 115g (4oz)
Egg yolk 75g (2½oz)
Whole egg 100g (3½oz)
Plain flour 45g (1½oz)
Cornflour 45g (1½oz)
Cocoa powder 30g (1oz)

Bake at 180°C (350°F), or gas mark 4, for approximately 15 minutes.

Filling:
Tia Maria
Double cream
Instant coffee (triple strength)

Decoration:
Grated chocolate and curls (see page 11)
Sieved icing sugar for dusting

ITEMS REQUIRED

2 sponge tins 20.5cm (8″) diameter
Greaseproof paper
Wire cooling tray
Waxed paper
Pastry brush

Eat within 24 hours

1 Set the oven to 180°C (350°F), or gas mark 4. Grease the 2 sponge tins with melted butter and dust with flour.

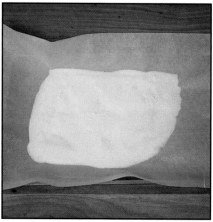

2 Place the sugar onto greaseproof paper and place in the oven to warm slightly, then pour into a mixing bowl.

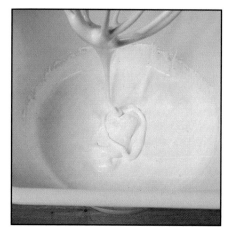

3 Whisk the yolks and whole egg into the warm sugar until the mixture becomes thick and creamy.

4 Sieve the dry ingredients together and fold into the creamed mixture.

5 Stir in the melted butter slowly. Divide the mixture equally between the 2 sponge tins and bake for approximately 15 minutes.

6 Remove sponges from the oven and leave for 5 minutes. Turn out and leave on a wire tray to cool. Wrap in waxed paper for 12 hours before use.

7 Using a brush, soak the sponges with Tia Maria.

8 Whip the fresh cream and beat in the instant coffee. Sandwich the 2 sponges together with a layer of cream. Cover the top and sides with remaining cream.

9 Cover the sponge with grated chocolate and curls (see page 11). Dust with icing sugar.

Chocolate and Brandy Fudge Cake

INGREDIENTS

Margarine 45g (1½oz)
Demerara sugar 130g (4½oz)
Egg 1 large
Couverture or compound chocolate 60g (2oz)
Plain flour 145g (5oz)
Bicarbonate of soda 1 level tsp
Salt – Large pinch
Milk 115g (4oz)
Liqueur of choice

Bake at 175°C (345°C), or gas mark 3½, for approximately 35 minutes.

Note: If using couverture in this recipe, it is not necessary to temper the chocolate.

Decoration:
Milk chocolate vermicelli 60g (2oz)
Milk chocolate triangles (see page 11)

Note: If using couverture for the chocolate triangles, the chocolate must be tempered (see page 8) OR, if using compound chocolate, this must be melted in the usual way (see page 9).

ITEMS REQUIRED

Loaf tin 680g (1½lb)
Greaseproof paper
Palette knife

Eat within 7 days

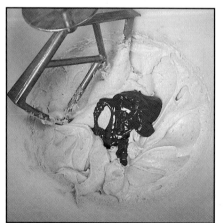

1 Grease the loaf tin and line the base and ends with greaseproof paper.

MAKING THE CAKE:

2 Place the margarine and sugar into a bowl and beat together well.

3 Gradually add the egg to the mixture and beat until light and creamy.

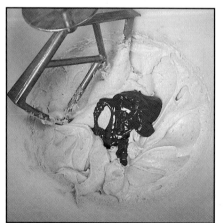

4 Melt the chocolate (see page 9) and mix it quickly into the cream.

5 Sieve the flour, salt and bicarbonate of soda together and add to the mixture. Stir in the milk and liqueur.

6 Pour the mixture into the prepared baking tin and bake at 175°C (345°F), or gas mark 3½, for approximately 35 minutes.

Cream Fudge Filling:
Butter 85g (3oz)
Sieved icing sugar 225g (8oz)
Double cream 3 tablespoons
Plain couverture or compound chocolate 75g (2½oz)
Brandy (optional)

Note: If using couverture in this recipe, it is not necessary to temper the chocolate.

Fudge Icing:
Plain couverture or compound chocolate 225g (8oz)
Double cream 170g (6oz)
Butter 45g (1½oz)

MAKING THE CREAM FUDGE FILLING:
7 Place the butter and icing sugar in a bowl and beat together until mixture is light and fluffy.

8 *Pour half the cream into the mixture and beat thoroughly.*

9 *Melt the chocolate and pour it into the creamed mixture. Immediately add the remaining cream and brandy (or other liqueur) and beat thoroughly.*

MAKING THE FUDGE ICING:
10 Break the chocolate into small pieces and place in a heat-proof bowl.

11 *Boil the cream and stir it into the chocolate pieces.*

12 *Add the butter to the mixture. Stir well and leave to cool.*

DECORATING THE CAKE:
13 Cut the fudge cake horizontally into 3 layers and sandwich together with the cream fudge filling.

14 Spread the fudge icing over the top of the cake with a palette knife, making the pattern shown.

15 Spread the remaining fudge filling around the sides and cover with milk vermicelli. Arrange the chocolate triangles along the top of the cake.

Chocolate Modelling Paste

Chocolate modelling paste is a versatile and easy-to-use medium for cake decorations. The paste can be prepared in advance and stored in a cool place as it keeps between four to six weeks.

Many attractive decorations can be quickly modelled as the paste holds its shape well. It can be cut with shaped cutters to form leaves, etc, or be moulded with the fingers to form flowers or figures.

INGREDIENTS
Compound chocolate 145g (5oz)
Warmed liquid glucose or corn syrup 115g (4oz)

ITEMS REQUIRED
Leaf-shaped cutter

1 Place the chocolate in a heat-proof bowl and melt in the usual way (see page 9).

2 Pour the warmed liquid glucose or corn syrup into the melted chocolate.

3 Stir the mixture with a wooden spoon until it becomes sticky.

4 Put the paste into a plastic bag or container and leave to set in a cool place for at least 12 hours. It is then ready for use.

5 Paste flowers and leaves can be made by building up individual petals (see page 68).

6 Chocolate paste figures can also be made. Features, such as eyes, may be piped in royal icing.

Chocolate Rose

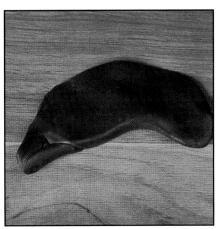

1 To make a chocolate paste rose bud, mould a small piece into the shape shown, using recipe from page 67.

2 Roll the paste over to form the rose bud. Trim as required.

3 To make a rose, take a bud and flatten its base. Stand it in an upright position to form the rose centre.

4 Mould a piece of paste into a ball and flatten it to form a petal.

5 Wrap the petal around the rose centre, curling its edges slightly, and press into place.

6 Make and fix one more petal.

7 Make and fix further petals until the rose is complete. Leave to dry for 24 hours. Make as many roses and buds as required for the cake.

8 To make the leaves, roll out the paste and cut with a leaf-shaped cutter, pressing firmly.

9 Draw the leaf veins with a sharp knife, or cocktail stick. Complete the leaves by curling their edges slightly. Leave to dry for 24 hours.

Chocolate Rose Cake

1 Arrange and fix the paste flowers and leaves (see pages 67-68) onto a coated heart-shaped cake.

2 Fill a piping bag with royal icing and pipe scrolls and inscription of choice onto the cake-top (No. 1).

3 Complete by piping plain shells around the base (No. 2). Then over-pipe outline on the shells (No. 1). Fix a spray of paste flowers to the base as shown.

Chocolate Swan Gateau

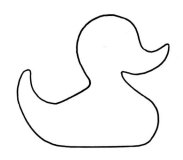

INGREDIENTS

Sponge:
Butter 225g (8oz)
Caster sugar 225g (8oz)
Eggs 6
Sieved plain flour 170g (6oz)
Cocoa powder 60g (2oz)
Baking powder 2 teaspoons
Pinch of salt
Brandy (optional)

Method:
Cream the butter and sugar. Slowly add the egg yolks and beat well. Whisk egg whites and add to the batter. Fold in dry ingredients and add brandy. Pour into 23cm (9″) round sponge tin.

Bake at 170°C (325°F), or gas mark 3, for approximately 1 hour.

ITEMS REQUIRED

Round sponge tin 23cm (9″) diameter
Cake board 30.5cm (12″) diameter
Serrated scraper
Templates
Waxed paper
Piping bag
Piping tube No. 13

Decoration:
Buttercream 680g (1½lb)
Couverture or compound chocolate 225g (8oz)
6 whole blanched almonds partially dipped in chocolate

Note: If using couverture for decorating, the chocolate must be tempered (see page 8) OR, if using compound chocolate, this must be melted in the usual way (see page 9)

Eat within 7 days

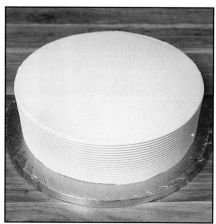

1 Make the sponge and leave to cool. Cut, fill and coat the sponge with buttercream using a serrated scraper around the sides. Place on a cake board.

2 Using the templates as a guide, pipe 6 pairs of swans and approximately 20 ducks in melted or tempered chocolate. Leave to set on waxed paper.

3 Spread chocolate onto waxed paper of a suitable size. Leave to set for 2 hours. Pipe a birthday inscription in buttercream.

4 *Pipe rosettes of buttercream around the top edge of the sponge (No. 13).*

5 *Top each rosette with a whole almond partially dipped in chocolate. Arrange the swans in pairs around alternate rosettes, as shown.*

6 *Fix the chocolate ducks closely together around the base of the sponge.*

Cherry and Kirsch Chocolate Ring

INGREDIENTS

Butter 225g (8oz)
Caster sugar 225g (8oz)
Plain couverture or compound chocolate 225g (8oz)
Sieved plain flour 170g (6oz)
Large eggs, separated 6
Apricot purée for glaze

Bake at 180°C (350°F), or gas mark 4, for approximately 45 minutes.

Note: If using couverture in this recipe, it is not necessary to temper the chocolate.

Filling:
Whole cherry jam
Kirsch

Coating:
Compound chocolate 340g (12oz)

Decoration:
Melted plain chocolate
Chocolate leaves (see page 11)

ITEMS REQUIRED

Cake ring, lightly greased with butter 23cm (9″)
Waxed paper
Wire cooling tray
Pastry brush
Savoy piping bag

Eat within 7 days

1 Melt the chocolate (see page 9). Cream the butter and sugar in a bowl and add the melted chocolate. Beat quickly until evenly mixed.

2 Add the flour to the mixture, a little at a time, alternating with egg yolk, until all yolk and flour have been used.

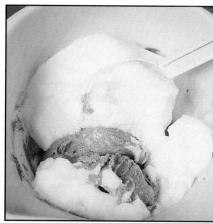

3 Whisk the egg whites in a separate grease-free bowl until firm, and gently fold into the creamed mixture.

4 Spread the mixture into the cake ring and bake at 180°C (350°F), or gas mark 4, for approximately 45 minutes.

5 Turn out sponge and leave to cool. Wrap in waxed paper for 12 hours. Slice the sponge and sprinkle the bottom layer with Kirsch. Spread with filling of choice.

6 Re-assemble the sponge. To glaze, boil the apricot purée in a saucepan and immediately brush it over the top and sides of the sponge.

7 Melt the compound chocolate (see page 8) and pour over the sponge.

8 Fill a piping bag with melted plain chocolate and pipe the filigree design on the top of the cake, as shown.

9 Complete the decoration by adding chocolate leaves (see page 11).

Round Novelty Sponge Cake

1 *Cover the top of a round sponge cake by coating with sugarpaste. Cover the sides with chocolate vermicelli.*

2 *Using piping chocolate (see page 55) pipe animal shapes onto waxed paper. Cover an un-set chocolate disc with vermicelli. Leave to set.*

3 *Fix animals around top edge of sponge. Place the disc in the centre and attach the rabbit. To complete, pipe shells of cream around the edge of the sponge (No. 7).*

Square Novelty Sponge Cake

1 Cover the top of a square sponge cake with sugarpaste. Cover the sides with grated chocolate or chocolate flakes.

2 Fill a bag with plain piping chocolate (see page 55). Pipe scrolls around the top edge of the cake (No. 43). Then pipe the lines shown (No. 2).

3 Use half an Easter egg as a boat. Pipe 'waves' and inscription of choice (No. 2). Make marzipan or sugarpaste figure, and oars from chocolate.

Tuille Gateau

INGREDIENTS

Tuille Biscuits:
Melted butter 60g (2oz)
Egg whites 2
Caster sugar 75g (2½oz)
Plain flour 60g (2oz)

Bake at 200 °C (400°F) or gas mark 6.

Makes approximately 20 biscuits

Dusting:
Icing sugar

Filling:
Orange and lemon buttercream
Orange liqueur

Coating:
Almond paste
Apricot purée
Chocolate flavoured fondant

Decoration:
Tuille biscuits
Cherries
Piping chocolate (see page 55)

ITEMS REQUIRED

Whisk
Two baking trays
Greaseproof paper
Chocolate sponge 20.5cm (10″) round
Cake board 30.5cm (12″) round
Sugar thermometer
Waxed paper

MAKING THE TUILLE BISCUITS:
1 Lightly whisk the egg whites in a clean, grease-free bowl.

2 Stir the sugar into the egg whites a little at a time.

3 Sift the flour into the mixture and gently fold it in using a metal spoon.

4 Gently fold the melted butter into the mixture.

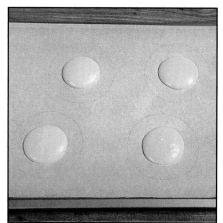

5 Line two baking trays with pure greaseproof paper, marking circles as shown. Spoon a small amount of mixture into the centre of each circle.

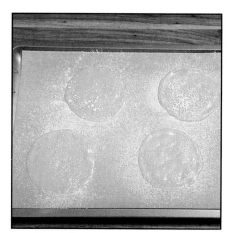

6 Using the back of the spoon, spread the mixture thinly and evenly to fill the circles. Dust lightly with sifted icing sugar.

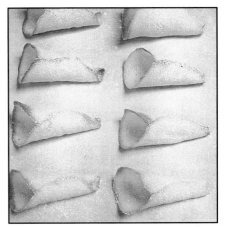

7 *Bake in the centre of a pre-heated oven for 5 minutes (or until pale brown at the edges). Meanwhile, prepare four more biscuits on the remaining baking tray.*

8 *Remove from oven and immediately roll the hot biscuit around a greased cone or cream horn tin. Bake and roll biscuits until all mixture is used.*

9 *As soon as the biscuits are crisp, slip them onto greaseproof paper and leave to cool. When cold, dust with icing sugar using a fine sieve.*

COATING THE SPONGE:

10 *Cut and fill the sponge with buttercream. Liqueur may be mixed into the buttercream or sprinkled onto the sponge beforehand.*

11 *Reassemble the sponge and coat the top and sides with buttercream. Place in a refrigerator for 1 hour.*

12 *Cover the coated sponge with a very thin layer of almond paste.*

13 *Boil the apricot purée in a saucepan and immediately brush a thin layer over the almond paste.*

14 *Place the sponge on a wire tray. Warm the chocolate flavoured fondant to 37°C (98°F) and pour it over the top of the sponge.*

15 *Using a palette knife, quickly spread the fondant to cover the top and side evenly. Place onto a cake board when set.*

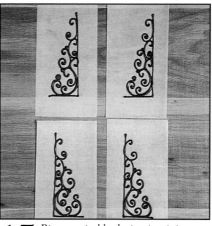

16 Fill each tuille biscuit with butter-cream and decorate with cherries. Arrange on top as shown. Pipe shells around the base.

17 Pipe a suitable design in piping chocolate (see page 55) onto waxed paper and allow to set.

18 Assemble the design carefully in an upright position to form a centrepiece. Place in centre of gateau to complete the decoration.

Chocolate Meringues

INGREDIENTS

Egg whites 3
Caster sugar 85g (3oz)
Icing sugar 85g (3oz)
Cocoa powder 30g (1oz)

Bake at 55°C (130°F), or gas mark ½, for 1-1¼ hours.

Decoration:
Melted chocolate compound

ITEMS REQUIRED

Egg whisk
Silicone paper or non-stick trays
Savoy piping bag
Savoy piping tubes

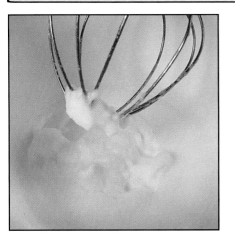

1 Using a grease-free bowl and whisk, thoroughly beat egg whites until light.

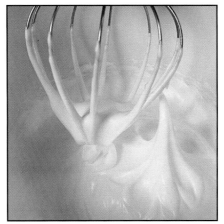

2 Gradually whisk the caster sugar into the egg whites then continually beat until the mixture is firm and stands up in peaks.

3 Sieve together the icing sugar and cocoa, and fold into the whisked egg whites.

4 Pipe mixture onto silicone paper or non-stick trays. Pipe stalks and caps for toadstools and then shells or other shapes as required.

5 Place trays in a cool oven at 55°C (130°F), or gas mark ½, for approximately 1-1¼ hours, or until crisp and dry.

6 Assemble toadstools using a little melted chocolate. Dust tops lightly with sieved icing sugar (see page 81). Use other shapes as required.

Chocolate Swiss Roll Log

INGREDIENTS

Eggs 2
Sugar 75g (2½oz)
Warm water 1 teaspoon
Plain flour 45gm (1½oz)
Cocoa powder 15gm (½oz)

Bake at 220°C (430°F), or gas mark 7, for approximately 8 minutes.

Makes 1 sponge (2 sponges are needed to make the chocolate log).

Coating:

Buttercream 455g (16oz)
Couverture or compound chocolate 455g (16oz)

Note: If using couverture, chocolate must be tempered before use (see page 8) OR, if using compound chocolate, this must be melted in the usual way (see page 9).

Decoration:

Royal icing
Seasonal decorations

Eat within 7 days

ITEMS REQUIRED

Swiss roll tin 30.5cm x 20.5cm (12″ x 8″)
Greaseproof paper
Pastry brush
Round cakeboard 35.5cm (14″)

1 Grease the swiss roll tin and line base and shorter sides with greased greaseproof paper.

2 Crack the eggs into a mixing bowl and stir in the sugar. Whisk until the mixture leaves a good trail as it drops from the whisk.

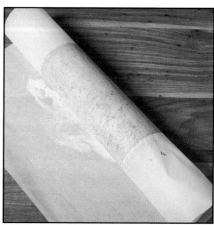

3 Stir in the warm water. Sieve together the flour and cocoa powder and fold into the egg mixture.

4 Spread the mixture into the prepared swiss roll tin and level the surface. Bake in the oven at 220°C (430°F), or gas mark 7, for approximately 8 minutes.

5 Remove from the oven and turn out onto greaseproof paper sprinkled with caster sugar. Leave to cool for 5 minutes.

6 Trim the edges and roll up the sponge with the paper, starting from short end. Keep tightly rolled until cold. Repeat steps 1 to 6 for a second sponge.

7 When the rolls are cold, unroll and spread with filling of choice, and re-roll. Coat the outside with cream and place in a refrigerator for 1 hour.

8 Cut and place the sponges on a board as shown. Using a brush, coat them with melted or tempered chocolate and mark with a fork to simulate bark.

9 Decorate the log and board with stippled royal icing, meringue toadstools (see page 79) and seasonal decorations, as shown.

Viennese Biscuits

INGREDIENTS

Butter 285g (10oz)
Caster sugar 85g (3oz)
Chocolate hazelnut spread 115g (4oz)
Lightly roasted ground almonds 60g (2oz)
Sieved plain flour 315g (11oz)

Bake at 175°C (345°F), or gas mark 3½,
for approximately 10 minutes.

Filling:
Buttercream 170g (6oz)
Chocolate hazelnut spread 2 tablespoons

Decoration:
Couverture or compound chocolate
Sieved icing sugar

Note: If using couverture, the chocolate must be tempered
(see page 8). If using compound chocolate, this must be
melted in the usual way (see page 9).

Makes 48 single biscuits.
Eat within 7 days.

ITEMS REQUIRED

Savoy piping bag
Plain savoy tube
Star savoy tube
Baking trays
Wire cooling tray
Waxed paper

1 Place all the ingredients together in a mixing bowl.

2 Beat the ingredients well to form a light, smooth mixture.

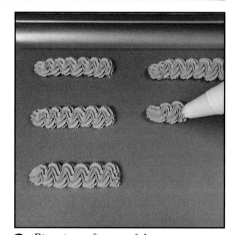

3 Pipe zigzag fingers of the mixture onto a lightly greased baking tray. Place in the oven and bake for approximately 10 minutes, or until golden brown.

4 Pipe rosettes of the mixture onto a separate, lightly greased baking tray and bake for approximately 10 minutes, or until golden brown.

5 Remove the fingers and rosettes from the baking trays and allow to cool on a wire tray.

6 Melt or temper the chocolate in the usual way (see pages 8 or 9) and dip each end of the finger biscuits, as shown. Leave to set on waxed paper for 1 hour.

7 Beat the hazelnut spread into the cream. Sandwich the finger biscuits together with the cream and additional hazelnut spread.

8 Sandwich pairs of rosettes together, as shown.

9 Sprinkle the rosettes with icing sugar and pipe fine lines of chocolate over the top to finish.

Chocolate Strawberry and Lime Flan

INGREDIENTS

Base:
Wheatmeal biscuits 170g (6oz)
Couverture or compound chocolate 85g (3oz)
Butter 30g (1oz)

Note: If using couverture in the base, it is not necessary to temper the chocolate.

Topping:
Marshmallows 400g (14oz)
Milk 145g (5oz)
Lime juice to taste

Filling and Decoration:
Strawberries 285-315g (10-12oz)
Whipped cream 85g (3oz)
Melted chocolate 170g (6oz)
Kiwi fruit
Chocolate cut-outs (see page 11)

ITEMS REQUIRED

Rolling pin
Flan ring with removeable base 20.5cm (8") diameter
Waxed paper

Eat within 2 days

MAKING THE BASE:

1 Using a rolling pin, crush the wheatmeal biscuits into fine crumbs.

2 Melt the chocolate and butter in a saucepan and stir with a wooden spoon.

3 Place the biscuit crumbs in a medium sized bowl and add the melted chocolate mixture. Mix thoroughly with a wooden spoon.

4 Lightly grease and line the inside of the flan ring with waxed paper. Spread the mixture evenly in the ring to make the biscuit base.

MAKING THE TOPPING:

5 Put the marshmallows and milk into a bowl and stand over a pan of hot water to melt the contents. Leave to cool.

6 Stir the lime juice into the cooled marshmallow mixture. Add the whipped cream and fold in carefully.

7 Arrange strawberries on the biscuit base and carefully spoon in the topping. Spread with a palette knife to make an even surface. Leave to set for 12 hours.

8 Gently remove the flan then peel away the waxed paper. Fix chocolate cut-outs around the flan side.

9 Decorate with rosettes of whipped cream, chocolate cut-outs, kiwi fruit and strawberries dipped in chocolate, as shown. Store in a refrigerator.

Dairy Cream Chocolate Ice

INGREDIENTS

Plain couverture or compound chocolate 170g (6oz)
Milk 285g (10oz)
Whole egg 1
Egg yolks 2
Caster sugar 85g (3oz)
Cornflour ½ teaspoon
Double cream 285g (10oz)

Note: If using couverture, it is not necessary to temper the chocolate.

ITEMS REQUIRED

Egg whisk
Plastic rectangular container 20.5 cm x 13cm x 7.5cm
    deep (8″ x 5″ x 3″)

Freeze for up to 3 months

1 Place the chocolate and milk in a saucepan. Warm over a low heat until the chocolate has melted, stirring continuously to form a smooth sauce.

2 Place the egg, egg yolks, sugar and cornflour in a bowl and beat together until light.

3 Pour in the warmed milk and chocolate mixture and whisk together until light.

4 Pour the mixture into a saucepan and stir over a low heat until it thickens slightly.

5 Pour the mixture through a sieve into a bowl. Allow to cool, giving an occasional stir.

6 Whip the cream in a separate bowl. DO NOT OVER-WHIP. Fold the cream into the cooled chocolate mixture.

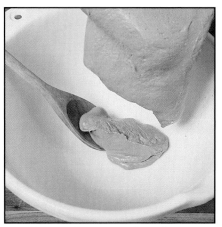

7 Pour the cream into a rectangular plastic container and place in a freezer for 1-1½ hours.

8 Remove the mixture from the container and place in a bowl. Using a wooden spoon, beat until smooth.

9 Pour into a container, cover and freeze until firm. Transfer to a fridge for 30 minutes before serving with wafers and chocolate leaves (see page 11).

Chocolate and Orange Mousse

INGREDIENTS

Filling:
Plain chocolate 115g (4oz)
Butter 15g (½oz)
Eggs, separated 4
Grated orange rind 2 teaspoons

Note: If using couverture in this recipe, it is not necessary to temper the chocolate.

Topping:
Double cream 285g (10oz)
Grated chocolate
Pared orange peel

ITEMS REQUIRED

6 fluted chocolate cases (see page 10)
Savoy piping bag
Star savoy tube
Grater

Makes 6 dishes
Eat within 24 hours

1 Make the 6 fluted chocolate dishes (see page 10).

MAKING THE FILLING:
2 Place the chocolate in a heat-proof bowl and melt in the usual way (see page 9). Remove the bowl from the heat and stir in the butter.

3 Gently stir in the egg yolks with a wooden spoon.

4 Add the grated orange rind to the chocolate mixture and stir thoroughly to mix.

5 Whisk the egg whites in a grease-free bowl until firm. Then carefully fold the whites into the chocolate mixture.

6 Spoon the mixture into the chocolate cases and leave in a refrigerator for 2 hours to set.

7 For the topping, whip the double cream and pipe a rosette onto each mousse-filled chocolate case.

8 Sprinkle grated chocolate over the cream, as shown.

9 To complete the topping, add a twist of finely pared orange peel. Serve immediately.

Chocolate Bakewell Tart

INGREDIENTS

Pastry case:
Plain flour 225g (8oz)
Salt ½ teaspoon
Margarine 50g (2oz)
Lard 50g (2oz)
Cold water 2-3 tablespoons

Method:
Sift together the flour and salt and rub in the fat until it resembles fine breadcrumbs. Add the water and combine to make a firm dough. Roll out to fit the sponge tin.

Filling:
Margarine 60g (2oz)
Caster sugar 60g (2oz)
Ground almonds 30g (1oz)
Egg 1
Almond essence ½ teaspoon
Finely grated rind of ½ lemon
Self-raising flour 60g (2oz)
Cocoa powder 1 tablespoon
Jam 3 tablespoons

Bake at 200°C (400°F), or gas mark 6, for 10 minutes, then at 180°C (350°F), or gas mark 4, for 15 minutes.

Topping:
Chocolate and white fondant

ITEMS REQUIRED

Round sponge tin 18cm (7″)
Wire cooling tray

Eat within 7 days

1 Make pastry and roll out and line the sponge tin. DO NOT STRETCH THE PASTRY.

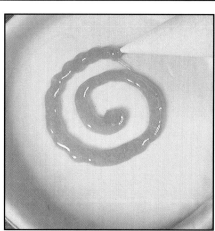

2 Starting in the centre, pipe jam onto the pastry base in a spiral shape.

3 Cream together the margarine and sugar and stir in the ground almonds. Beat in the egg and add the almond essence and grated lemon rind.

4 Sieve together the flour and cocoa powder and lightly fold into the creamed mixture.

5 Spread the mixture evenly in the prepared pastry case. Bake at 200°C (400°F), or gas mark 6, for 10 minutes then reduce to 180°C (350°F), or gas mark 4, for 15 minutes.

6 Remove from the oven and leave in the tin to cool.

7 When cool, remove from the tin and place on a wire tray. Brush the surface with jam.

8 Warm the chocolate and white fondant to 37°C (98°F). Immediately pour the chocolate fondant over the surface of the tart.

9 Before the chocolate sets, pipe the white fondant in circles on top. Draw up the lines using a sharp knife to create 'feather icing'. Leave to set for 1 hour.

Profiteroles

INGREDIENTS

Butter 60g (2oz)
Water 115g (4oz)
Plain flour 60g (2oz)
Pinch of salt
Egg 225g (8oz)

Bake at 200°C (400°F), or gas mark 6, for approximately 10-15 minutes.

Filling:
Fresh cream, custard or ice-cream

Chocolate Sauce:
Plain chocolate 225g (8oz)
Water 225g (8oz)
Rum, or flavour of choice 1 tbsp
Butter 100g (3½oz)

Note: If using couverture, it is not necessary to temper the chocolate.

ITEMS REQUIRED

Baking tray
Savoy piping bag
Plain savoy tube
Wire cooling tray

MAKING THE PROFITEROLES:
1 Melt the butter and water in a saucepan, and bring to the boil.

2 Whilst still on the heat, stir in the flour and salt as quickly as possible. Continue stirring for 1 minute.

3 Remove from the heat and stir the paste vigorously for approximately 2 minutes, until it leaves the sides of the saucepan.

4 Beat in the egg, a little at a time, until all the egg is used.

5 Using the savoy bag and tube, pipe small bulbs of mixture onto a lightly greased baking tray.

6 Bake in the centre of the oven for 10-15 minutes until golden brown. Leave to cool on a wire tray. Deep freeze until required.

MAKING THE CHOCOLATE SAUCE:

7 Cut the chocolate into small chips and place in the saucepan with the water and rum (or flavour of choice).

8 Slowly bring the mixture to the boil, stirring frequently until the sauce is smooth. Remove from the heat.

9 Add the butter and stir until the butter melts and the sauce is smooth. Leave to cool. Serve with cream-filled profiteroles.

Chocolate Fudge Tartlets

INGREDIENTS

Sweetpaste Pastry:
Sieved plain flour 255g (9oz)
Lard 170g (6oz)
Sugar 75g (2½oz)
Egg yolk 1

Method:
Rub the fat into the flour until it resembles fine breadcrumbs. Dissolve the sugar in the egg yolk and combine it with the fat and flour to make a firm dough. Leave to stand in a refrigerator overnight before cutting into rounds. Bake blind in foil cases at 200°C (400°F), or gas mark 6, for 10 minutes.

Filling:
Butter 60g (2oz)
Caster sugar 227g (8oz)
Evaporated milk 85g (3oz)
Vanilla essence
Jam 60g (2oz)
Melted chocolate 115g (4oz)
Fondant 455g (16oz)

Note: If using couverture, it is not necessary to temper the chocolate.

Topping:
Fresh whipped cream
Chocolate curls

ITEMS REQUIRED

18 tarts in foil cases
Wire cooling tray
Sugar thermometer
Piping bag

Makes 18 tarts
Eat within 24 hours

1 Make the tartlets in foil cases (see method above) and stand on a wire tray to cool.

2 Pipe or spoon the jam around the base of each tartlet.

MAKING THE FILLING:

3 Heat all the ingredients together in a saucepan until the sugar dissolves. Boil the mixture until a temperature of 116°C (240°F) is reached.

4 Remove the pan from the heat and pour the fudge mixture into a bowl. Stir until cool and slightly thick.

5 Fill a piping bag with the cooled fudge and pipe it into each tartlet, covering the jam.

6 Melt the chocolate in the usual way (see page 9). Warm the fondant to 38°C (100°F) and add the melted chocolate.

7 Top each tartlet with a spoonful of the chocolate fondant, covering the tops completely.

8 Pipe a rosette of fresh cream over the top of each tartlet.

9 Make chocolate curls (see page 11) and complete the topping by adding them to the sides of the cream.